MISTER BOFFO

UNCLEAR ON THE CONCEPT

MISTER BOFFO

UNCLEAR ON THE CONCEPT

Joe Martin

LITTLE, BROWN AND COMPANY   BOSTON / TORONTO / LONDON

FIRST EDITION

Library of Congress Cataloging-in-Publication Data

Martin, Joe, 1945–
     Mister Boffo : unclear on the concept / Joe Martin.
        p.   cm.
     ISBN 0-316-54859-6
     I. Title.   II. Title: Mister Boffo.
     PN6728.M7M37   1989
     741.5'973—dc19
                                              88-35550
                                                 CIP

10 9 8 7 6 5 4 3 2 1

RRD - VA

DESIGNED BY JEANNE ABBOUD

Published simultaneously in Canada
by Little, Brown & Company (Canada) Limited

PRINTED IN THE UNITED STATES OF AMERICA

A Time to Worry about People Unclear on the Concept

Dear Mr. Boffo,

I read your comic every day and I never thought I'd be writing you for advice, but my sister-in-law and her husband came for a visit last Christmas and still haven't left.... What should I do!??

Crowded in L.A.

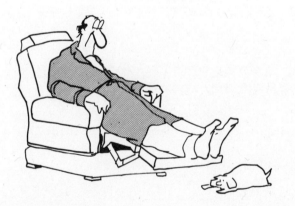

Dear Mister Martin,

My husband and I are going through a difficult period right now and I'm wondering if you might do more jokes on shoes?

Imelda (and Ferd)
xoxoxo

Dear Mr. Boffo,

I broke up with my boyfriend six months ago, and even though I made it clear I never want to see him again, he calls me whenever he doesn't get one of your jokes. Is there any possible way I can give him your phone number?

Troubled in Toledo,
Tess

Dear Mr. Martin, Esq.,

Your cartoon depicting a man being executed in the electric chair while holding two pieces of toast is the most inexcusable, tasteless, callous attempt at humor Miss Manners has ever seen.

It is obvious that the toast is for the warden and the guard . . . but what about the witnesses? The chaplain? The reporters and all the other invited guests? A little consideration of others and a little etiquette would go a long way.

Miss Manners

Dear Dad,

I read Mr. Boffo every day and it really hits home. The characters are like people I really know . . . crazy aunts, odd uncles. It's like you're looking over my shoulder every minute. I don't know how you do it, but keep it up!

Sincerely,
Your son, Jay

Dear Cartoonist,

When I first started reading Mr. Boffo I had a lopsided coffee table, but I've been clipping out my favorites and putting them under the leg and it's no longer wobbly. Thanks for making my life a little better.

Sincerely yours,
Steady Reader in Cincinnati

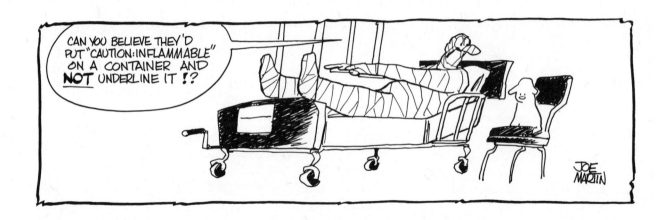

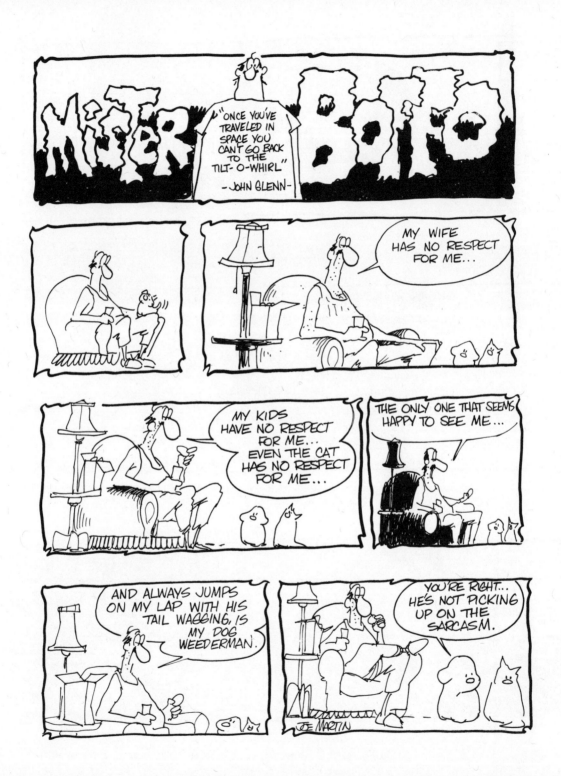

MISTER BOFFO AND HIS WONDER-DOG "WEEDERMAN"

"ONCE YOU CAN ACCEPT THE UNIVERSE AS MATTER EXPANDING INTO NOTHING THAT IS SOMETHING, WEARING STRIPES WITH PLAID COMES EASY"
—EINSTEIN ON CLOTHES—

AS A SAFEGUARD FOR THE SECURITY OF OUR NATION...IN ORDER TO INITIATE A NUCLEAR ATTACK...

JOE MARTIN

FIVE MEN AT FIVE SEPARATE LOCATIONS MUST PUSH FIVE SEPARATE BUTTONS...

AND PULL FIVE SEPARATE LEVERS...

SIMULTANEOUSLY.

THIS IS THE STORY OF THOSE FIVE MEN...

KABOOM

"HANDCUFFED TO THE BARS OF A CARDBOARD PRISON,
HE WAITS OUT HIS TIME LIKE THE FOOL HE IS"

ALSO RANS

SMELL NO EVIL   EAT NO EVIL   STEP ON NO EVIL   CHEW NO EVIL   SPIT NO EVIL

WYATT EARP, DOC HOLLIDAY
AND BAT MASTERSON,
BORN TOO LATE

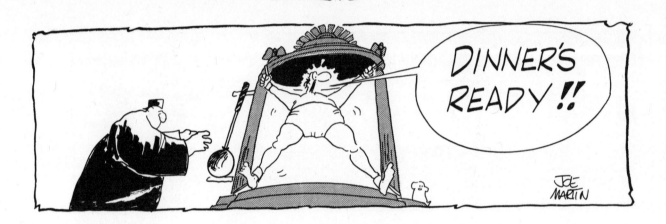

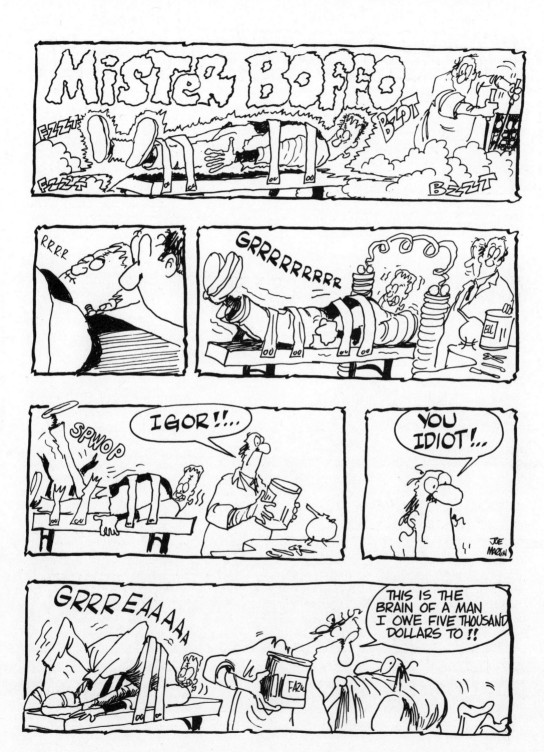